HANDBOOKS OF EUROPEAN NATIONAL DANCES

EDITED BY
VIOLET ALFORD

DANCES OF GREECE

Plate 1
Epirote costume

DANCES of GREECE

DOMINI CROSFIELD

NOVERRE PRESS

ILLUSTRATED BY
DOREEN RENBOLD
AFTER DRAWINGS BY
ATHENA TARSOULI
MUSIC ARRANGED FOR THE PIANO BY
FERDINAND RAUTER

First published in 1948
This edition published in 2020 by
The Noverre Press
Southwold House
Isington Road
Binsted
Hampshire
GU34 4PH

ISBN 978-1-906830-93-9

© 2020 The Noverre Press

CONTENTS

	Page
INTRODUCTION	7
Continuity of Tradition	8
Remains of Ritual Drama	9
The Circular Dance	10
Men's Circular Dances	11
Maidens' Dance	13
Syrtos—Kalamatianos	14
A Tragic Circle	15
Music	16
Costume	17
WHEN DANCING MAY BE SEEN	21
THE DANCES	22
Abbreviations	22
Poise of the Body and Holds	23
Basic Steps	23
Pentozali	24
Kalamatianos	27
Tsamikos	32
Hassapikos	36
BIBLIOGRAPHY	40

Illustrations in Colour, pages 2, 19, 30, 31
Map of Greece, page 6

INTRODUCTION

I T is difficult to trace the beginnings of dancing in Greece, for from the age of mythology down to the present time the Greeks have recorded their joys, their tragedies and their wars in song and dance.

At Knossos, in Crete, where Sir Arthur Evans brought to light the amazing treasures of the Minoan Age, youths and maidens took part in the religious rites, and welcomed the coming of Spring with dance. It is on this island that the Hymn of the Kuretes—armed ritualistic dancers—was discovered, invoking the Spring, telling each other to 'leap for full jars and fleecy flocks' exactly as Russian girls leap for the hemp to grow today. At the feasts of Demeter, at those of Hera and Artemis, and at the Panathenaic Festival for Athena, maidens danced in long robes, and at Delos dancers came from distant States to honour the god, for in ancient days dancing was an important part of the religion of the people. With the coming of Christianity it still was used in the early Church, for presently we find dancing forbidden during the Liturgy. But vestiges of these rites still survive as we can see today in the Greek Orthodox Church, where during the Christmas and Easter Services, and at marriage feasts, the priests move in a circle round the altar chanting the Liturgy.

In Homer we find repeated allusions to dancing, expressing warlike exultation and feelings of love and joy, but the apogee of dancing was reached in the Classical Age, when over two hundred religious, athletic, dramatic and popular dances were performed in the theatre, the stadium and the temple, and the Muse of the Dance, Terpsichore, was loved and honoured.

Plato extolled dancing. In his opinion 'The uneducated man is not likely to have the ability to dance; on the other hand the man of education must be considered perfectly apt to do so.'

CONTINUITY OF TRADITION

Of these ancient dances, we can trace about thirty which through the ages have come down to the present day, and if we look at the ancient vase paintings and bas-reliefs, we find that the poise, the steps and motions are very similar to those in the Greek dances of today. For the dance is a national tradition, and though it may have undergone changes its fundamental lines remain the same. One finds in modern Greek popular dances the greatest diversity of rhythms and combinations of rhythms, and consequently of steps and figures.

To quote Dr. Stephanides, a Greek authority: '. . . in Greece folk poetry continued quietly to exist by the side of its rival (the cultured Muse) and to retain its vitality in the mouth and memory of the people. Folk songs are still declaimed, sung or danced to, with few variations since the last thousand years, in all the lands inhabited by the Greeks.'

We also find that although the music has to a certain extent been influenced by the invasion of other peoples, it still retains the characteristic 7/8 and 5/4 beats.

Today in every village and town, on the mainland, in the Islands, and even in Asia Minor, ancient Greek territorial feasts, anniversaries, family rejoicings are all accompanied by dancing and song. The small village has its dancing place,

Chorostasi, and even the monasteries have a special ground for dancing purposes. The dancers sing either in chorus or individually, and are generally accompanied by local instruments. Each province in Greece has its local dance; not only are these typical of the region in which they are practised, but the text of the poem and the movements of the body also show regional characteristics. For example, let us look at a Pair dance, the Ballos, perhaps of Venetian origin, introduced when, after the Fourth Crusade, Venetians occupied the country. It comes from the Ionian Islands, should be danced by eight couples at once, and its foundation, like that of so many Pair dances, is somewhat erotic in character.

REMAINS OF RITUAL DRAMA

We must also glance at two remnants of ritual, possibly of Dionysiac ritual, as archaic as the Circular dance ånd as important in the great field of Indo-European custom—the Springtime Death and Resurrection dance-drama, and that queer survival the Hobby Horse.

Greece possesses many examples on her Thracian borders of the Death and Resurrection Play enacted during Carnival, of which the English Mummers' Play is a living and famous example. The island of Skyros boasts a variant in which figure the usual folk characters, the Man-Woman in bridal attire, the Animal-masker in skins, laden with fifty or sixty sheep bells which clash deafeningly as he leaps—'the purpose of the leaping and dancing is solely to evoke as much noise as possible from the bells... the interior of a belfry with a peal being rung would be peace and quiet after the jar and jangle of hundreds of these goat-bells when the troupe of dancers wheel suddenly round some corner and pour past down the rugged, slippery road, or at the end of the dance leap together into the air and come together with a crash...'*

* G. C. Lawson. *Annual of the British School at Athens*, No. VI, p. 127.

The Thracian plays show more drama and less dance, if such leaping can be called by that name, but show the same Animal-guise and two 'Brides', as well as the widely known Old Woman carrying the bastard babe. The all-important Spring ploughing is duly performed, a phallus-bearing ritualist somehow becomes the bastard now grown up, who is married to one of the 'Brides', shot, lamented, and brought to life again. In these dance-dramas we find the age-old Spring rite duly performed in the proper season.

Another means of bringing in 'the Summer and the May O' is the appearance of the Carnival Hobby Horse, even in the streets of Athens. He is festooned with paper streamers, and his rider, an Attic peasant in black cap and snowy foustanella, canters and dances on his own legs, but displays a pair of rider's false legs cunningly hung on either side of the horse-body. His accompanying music is a strange little tune played by an attendant piper.*

THE CIRCULAR DANCE

To return to the Circular dance, a closed circle or an open one which becomes a chain like the Southern French Farandole—which indeed is claimed as a descendant of an ancient Greek dance through the Greek colonists who founded what is now Marseilles. The word Choros, χορός, meant and still means both a chorus and a dance, and like the circular dancing place (which originally was nothing more than a country threshing-floor) whereon the Choros circled in the great tragedies of Aeschylus, Sophocles and Euripides, is still found, as we have just noted, in the Chorostasi of even the smallest village. Homer in the *Iliad* describes the Cyclic (circular) dance in which men only took part. The musicians, pipers and players of the lyre, stood in the centre of the circle; the women looked on the spectacle with rapture from the windows of the surrounding houses. Today—after

* Violet Alford and Rodney Gallop. *The Traditional Dance*, p. 152.

some 5,000 years or so—women have begun to dance occasionally with the men, but as a rule they still look on from the windows as their men compete for the honours of the dance.

There is the closed Circular dance with hands joined, the Klephtikos (Dance of the Klephts, or Mountain Warriors), the Hassapikos (Dance of the Butchers), and the Syrtos, which is popular in most of the Islands and is supposed to be a survival of the Old Pyrrhic of which more presently. But the Greek National Dance today is the Kalamatianos. One of the dancers leads, singing and waving a handkerchief aloft; from time to time he detaches himself from the group to perform intricate swirls and jumps named *scherza*. The introduction of the scherza arises naturally out of the monotony of the continuous chain of the Choros. When he is exhausted, the first leader throws the handkerchief to another, who takes the lead in his turn. The dancers generally sing in chorus accompanied by the lyre, essentially a Greek instrument which has come down to us from classical times, or by guitars, mandolines, clarinets and drums. At weddings in Cyprus and other lands inhabited by Greeks, the Dance of the Wedding Dress is performed by the bridesmaids, and the Dance of the Bridal Pair by the new couple, during which the guests throw gold and silver coins and notes on to a salver, or pin valuable cloths or silk handkerchiefs on to the bridegroom's shoulder, these forming the wedding gifts which each has to offer.

MEN'S CIRCULAR DANCES

In spite of the long occupation of Greece, the Turks did not wholly succeed in subjecting the Greek population. The young Greek Klephts (guerrillas) preferred to take refuge in the mountains, where they lived in freedom waging incessant warfare against their foes, similar to that which was waged during the German occupation. They cut the enemy communications and carried off prisoners and booty; they also protected the villages against assault by Turkish bands and marauders, and a large number of historical ballads describing their heroic deeds exists today. Their dances were circular, but of a martial character, performed only by men; the steps were usually accompanied by the brandishing of naked sabres, or later by the firing of pistols into the air. These warlike dances are still practised in Greece today.

The Tsamikos is again of martial character, and is danced by guerrillas on their way down the mountains to battle. With stamps, leaps and cries of 'Oppa!' the men vie with each other, especially when women are watching, in intricacy of steps and nobility of demeanour.

I must mention the Mirologhia, which are dancing songs composed for the dead. They are of an austere and imposing character. To quote P. J. Petrides: 'While a soldier in the Balkan wars I witnessed one of the Mirologhia danced by the Evzones, the Greek Light Infantry. They had just gone through some very heavy fighting. Out of some 800 of their battalion, hardly 50 were left alive. Their beloved commander, whom they used to call *O Mavros*—the Black One—was among the fallen. When night came, they laid the dead chief on a couch about two feet high, made of branches and leaves, lit big fires all round, and started singing and dancing a Mirologhi. I do not remember having seen anything approaching this scene of savage poetry and picturesqueness. The closing scene of the *Walkyrie* does not contain half as much intense life as burst forth from that sight I witnessed on a Macedonian mountain peak.'

The Chaniotiko, from Canea, Crete, another Circular dance, is claimed as a descendant of the Pyrrhic, the dance preparatory to battle, and should be accompanied with clarinet and small drum. In this dance the tail of the *vraka*, the exaggeratedly full breeches which hang down between the legs in a 'tail', should come into play. The Cretans wear a long white calico shirt under the vraka, and this stuffed well in fills out the tail and gives it weight for swinging. But much more popular in Crete is the Pentozali, described later.

The Sousta—created, tradition tells us, by Pyrrhos, son of Achilles—is supposed to have been danced round the pyre of Patroklos by Achilles. According to G. Sakellariou, this dance was representative of the movements of warriors in full armour with shield and spear. In the seventh century it became one of Sparta's chief military exercises, and was taught to children from the age of five. From the sixth century onward, it was danced in Athens at the Panathenaic Festival, while Plato in *The Laws* refers to this dance as excelling all others, even describing it in detail. The dancers are said to represent by their movements the various stages in the contest—the beat of marching feet, the din of clashing arms. According to Athenaeus, women began to dance the Pyrrhic from about A.D. 300 when it dissolved into a Pair dance, and love instead of war became its motif. Centuries later it is heard of but confined to a few islands in the Aegean, particularly Crete, where local names were given it. And still it lives. The modern descendant of the Sousta is danced principally in Crete, has lost its martial character and again becomes a Pair dance with a love motif, man and woman facing each other. The dance leaves much to the initiative of the individual and is therefore danced only by the best dancers. The steps are not well defined but are governed largely by the temperament and mood of the performer. One or two couples dance at a time.

MAIDENS' DANCE

The Trata, the Maidens' Dance at Megara, is a Chain dance performed only at Easter, the village girls wearing their best dresses, their caps covered with little silver coins. They sing their own dance tune, and, linking hands crossed over their bodies in front, circle slowly to right and left, monotonously but impressively all the same.

SYRTOS—KALAMATIANOS

The ancient dance Syrtos is described in great detail by Lucian, in his chapter on dances. Youths and maidens danced it in a circle. The man who led the dance executed complicated steps to display his youthful valour; demure maidens followed, hand upon wrist. This is still popular in the Islands, but today the ancient Syrtos has become the Kalamatianos, and under the newer name has become a real Greek national dance. It is still danced in a circle; the man leading the dance performs various swirls, turns and jumps. He makes fencing lunges, as if he held a sword, while the girls follow holding hands. They are described in a popular ballad as 'willowy and of downcast eyes; in fact demure'.

This and its older Syrtos form are the favourites of the Evzones, the 'beautifully belted ones', when they gather at the cafés and drinking places they like to patronise. The music at such a place is provided by a fiddle, a bulging mandoline and a zither, played by a gipsy. You hand over a small sum to the band, and proceed to form your chain linked by handkerchiefs or hands, and call the tune. The Evzones are recruited from all over Greece so there is a good variety of steps, and the Kalamatianos makes a good background on which to embroider. The foundation step continues all the time as the chain moves round, while the outstanding dancers indulge not only in real virtuosity but in gymnastic feats and extraordinary tricks, always keeping in place and in time. One man was seen to hold his beer mug by his lips alone, and swallow his drink thus as he spun round and round or leapt into the air.* This could hardly improve the beauty of the old dance, but others, especially the leader, waving a handkerchief in rhythmic swirls, often give a wonderful display of improvised steps.

* Violet Alford and Rodney Gallop. *The Traditional Dance*, p. 152.

A TRAGIC CIRCLE

The Kalamatianos is often performed to the song of Zalongo, that tragic and historical ballad recounting an episode of the Turkish occupation of Epirus.

In the year 1802 the most oppressed Greek province was Epirus, famous in antiquity for its arts and sciences. It was ruled by an Albanian tyrant, Ali Pasha, so bloodthirsty that the Sultan's yoke in other parts of Greece appeared lenient in comparison with his. Treachery, torture and murder were the weapons of this bandit chief from the wild Moslem tribes of Central Albania. Having murdered his benefactors and those of his own kin who stood in his way, Ali reigned supreme over Yannina, the Greek city renowned for its scholars and its cultured merchants, its seminaries and Greek schools.

However, there was one thorn in the flesh of this Albanian despot, one obstacle to his lust for power. The Confederation of Highland villages of Souli, which throughout 350 years of Ottoman domination over Greece had never submitted to the Sultan, refused to recognise his rule. Ali sent expeditions against their fastnesses, but the courage of the mountain folk managed to repel them each time. The walled villages of Souli were in a continuous state of siege; women fought by the side of their men and were well trained in the use of firearms. Eventually the Pasha appealed for a truce and a treaty of peace was signed, but the men of Souli were led into a trap and all were killed or captured. On learning this fearful news, their womenfolk decided to die rather than fall into the hands of the Moslem Albanians. On 23rd December 1803, these proud Highland amazons found themselves besieged on the mountain of Zalongo, with their ammunition running short. When at length no bullets were left for their red-hot guns, the Souliote women, inspired by the daughter of the Chieftain, the twenty-one-year-old Helena Botzaris, put on for the last time their festal costumes of crimson velvet and gold and, forming the antique circle of their forefathers, danced a last, memorable dance, singing:

> *Farewell, unhappy world, farewell sweet life;*
> *Farewell, farewell forever, our poor Country.*
>
> *Farewell, ye mountain springs, vales, hills and cliffs.*
> *Farewell, farewell forever, our poor Country.*
>
> *The fish cannot live on dry land,*
> *Nor the blossom in the salted sand of the beach,*
> *And the women of Souli cannot live without liberty.*
> *The women of Souli descend into Hades—the free*
>   *city of death—*
> *With festal dance and songs of joy.*

With despair in their hearts the women threw their children over the great cliff of Zalongo, and after this first immolation each tragic revolution of the circle claimed its victim. One by one as the great chain turned, in their gorgeous crimson they leapt to their deaths, till Helena Botzaris stood on the edge alone. One more supreme effort, and that tiny crimson and gilded figure hurtled into the abyss.

MUSIC

Although up to now Greek dances have not to any extent inspired our modern composers, Petro Petrides has produced at the Greek National Theatre *The Pedlars*, an attractive ballet, in which he has made use of many Greek dances and songs.

The ancient Greek chorus was full of meaning, making choral what was merely dramatic. This character has been preserved in the Greek folk dances of today. Dance songs are usually sung in unison by many voices—the chorus being still the dancers themselves. Tunes are entirely melodic, and attempts to harmonise them for popular orchestration are clumsy and not successful. Modern Greek instruments used today are the bagpipes in the North, the lute, a guitar, a reed pipe and various types of drum. Sometimes the clarinet appears and a peculiar violin called *Kritiki Lyra*, the Cretan Lyre, played with a bow. The main characteristic of the dance music is, as has been said, the great diversity of rhythms ranging from 7/8 and 5/8 to the more common 3/8 and 2/4 measures.

COSTUME

Every province has its own traditional costume handed down from generation to generation, to be worn on festive occasions. Greece possesses costumes representing all epochs, from ancient Byzantine days up to the present time.

Until quite recently and even at the present time in the Islands, Epirus and Macedonia, peasant women not only made their own clothes and linen, but prepared their own dyes. They were self-sufficient for the ordinary needs of life; they grew their own flax for linen and their silk was obtained from the home-bred silkworm, not from silk factories and shops.

Embroideries occupy a peculiar place in the social economy of the people of the Greek Islands. They are real folk embroideries, made by the women for their own household purposes with no intention of sale.

In Epirus, women's dress (Plate 1) is of hand-woven white material, the apron embroidered in red and black wool or silk. This embroidery appears also on the border of the long felt jacket. The full sleeves of the blouse show beneath the short sleeves of this jacket. A short waistcoat embroidered with gold or coloured thread is worn beneath the jacket. The head-dress is a gauze scarf, fringed, or with gold tinsel edging; sometimes a flat felt cap with massive tassel is seen. Men wear a black scarf rolled turban-wise round their heads, or, as in Macedonia, a red felt fez. These costumes would be correct for the Tsamikos.

Perhaps the most attractive of all these costumes is the foustanella, worn notably by the Evzones, the celebrated Greek Guards. Their dress uniform is composed of a full-sleeved, white shirt, embroidered cloth bolero of dark-blue, long white woollen stockings, bright red shoes with huge black pom-poms on the upturned toes (which by no means interfere with the agility of the wearer), and a full, pleated, snow-white skirt, the foustanella, measuring some 40 yards round. At the beginning and end of the dance, use is made of the swing of this full skirt and of the toss of the wide sleeve of the shirt. No heels are worn in any of these dances. Plate 4.

The most decorative of women's costumes is the Amalia, originally worn at the Court of the first King of Greece—King Otho—and Queen Amalia, from whom the dress gets its name. This is a full, ankle-length skirt, with white blouse and heavily embroidered bolero. Sometimes an ornamental buckle is worn at the waist. A trace of Turkish influence remains in the small red cap with its long and heavy silk tassel resembling the fez worn by the Turks. This is a Court and urban dress and can be properly worn in any dance. Plate 3.

The Cretan costume is usually a plain white shirt, blue or crimson sash, white top-boots, a blue and white braid-embroidered waistcoat with cloak thrown over the shoulder, and a black vraka (full breeches). The woman's dress is very similar to that of the Epirote women. Plates 2 and 1.

Women wear as headgear multi-coloured silk scarves and handkerchiefs; in Attica these are swathed round the head with rows of coins across the brow. In Euboea scarves are worn loosely round the throat, the ends hanging over the shoulders. The Corfu women wear a high, starched, white linen cap; in Macedonia a small, peaked felt cap with a fringed veil hanging from the peak and a posy of flowers tucked over one ear. Remarkable are the strings of silver or gold coins, or sometimes coloured beads, round their necks. A rich bride is recognised by the number and wealth of these.

Plate 2
Cretan costume

NOTE

We beg you not to think of regional costumes as fancy dress. They are held in honour by their wearers as an important part of their heritage. Respect them. Do not dress dancers in a make-believe foustanella for the Cretan dances. You would be equally justified in dressing a Helston Furry dancer in a Highland kilt.

The Editor

FESTIVALS AND SEASONS WHEN DANCING MAY BE SEEN

New Year's Day.
Feast of the Annunciation—March 25th.
Carnival season—Anywhere, town or country.
Easter—Especially the Trata, the Maidens' Dance, at Megara on Easter Tuesday.
Feast of the Assumption—August 15th.
St. Nicholas's Day—December 6th.

Every village keeps its own festival on the day of its Patron Saint, generally the Saint to whom the church is dedicated.

SCHOOLS OF DANCING

Madame Pratsika's School of Dancing, Athens.
Royal National Theatre, Athens.
G. Sakellariou. Academy of Dancing.

AUTHORITIES ON DANCING AND FOLKLORE

Le Lykeion des Dames Grecques, Athens.
Musée des Arts Decoratifs, Athens.
Historical and Ethnological Museum, Athens.

THE DANCES

TECHNICAL EDITOR, MURIEL WEBSTER
ASSISTED BY KATHLEEN P. TUCK

*ABBREVIATIONS
USED IN DESCRIPTION OF THE STEPS AND DANCES*

r—right } referring to R—right } describing turns or
l—left } hand, foot etc. L—left } ground pattern
C—clockwise   C-C—counter-clockwise

For descriptions of foot positions and explanations of any ballet terms the following books are suggested for reference:

A Primer of Classical Ballet (Cecchetti method). Cyril Beaumont.

First Steps. Ruth French and Felix Demery.

The Ballet Lover's Pocket Book. Kay Ambrose.

REFERENCE BOOKS FOR DESCRIPTION OF FIGURES:

The Scottish Country Dance Society's Publications. Many volumes, from Thornhill, Cairnmuir Road, Edinburgh 12.

The English Folk Dance and Song Society's Publications. Cecil Sharp House, 2 Regent's Park Road, London N.W.1.

The Country Dance Book I–VI. Cecil J. Sharp. Novello & Co., London.

POISE OF THE BODY AND HOLDS

The poise of the body is dignified and upright. The characterisation varies slightly according to the sex and type of the dancers. The Evzones carry themselves proudly, and work the dances up with movements of great vigour and spring. The Klephts or guerrillas have a more stealthy movement, as in Tsamikos, but they also spring and turn, whereas the women in all the dances have a much smoother movement with very little elevation even in a hopping step, and they never vary the basic movement as do the men dancers—'in fact demure'.

As many of the dances are done in a circular or chain formation, arm gestures are practically excluded. The usual grasp is the ordinary hand grasp, but sometimes the dancers hold each other by the wrist or hold the handkerchief of the next dancer. In certain dances, the Cretan for example, a shoulder grasp is usual. The leader uses his handkerchief as he likes, and often leaves the chain and dances singly.

BASIC STEPS AND GROUND PATTERN

These consist of steps in a sideways, forward or backward direction, and include hopping movements. The predominant feature of the dances is the variation of rhythm in slow and quick steps. Most of the dances work up either in speed as in the Cretan, or in the amount of springing and turning movements by the men as in Tsamikos.

The ground pattern is varied according to the will of the leader, who may join up with the last dancer to form a circle. The chain may be broken up during the dance into small circles but it probably finishes in the chain formation, as in the Cretan dance. Men and women do not generally dance together except perhaps in a small village. More usual is a chain of either men or women, although one man sometimes leads a chain of women and another man might form the tail.

PENTOZALI. *Cretan Dance*

Region Crete. The dance is mainly performed by men. Plate 2.

Character Springy and energetic—working up to a great speed.

Formation Starts in a chain, the dancers with hands on each other's shoulders. The chain may break into small chains but the dancers usually finish in one line, and dance on the spot when the music is at its fastest. The movement is mainly to the R, counter-clockwise direction.

Dance. Feet together, toes to centre.

MUSIC
Bar 1

1 Step l, hop on l, swinging r leg across with a straight knee.

Beats: 1
& 2

Bar 2

2 Spring on r swinging l leg across.
Turning to R, spring on l and step forward on r in front of l, facing the line of dance.
Turning to L, pivot on r foot.

Beats: 1
& 2

Bar 3

3 Step back on l backing the line of dance, spring on r turning to face the line of dance and step forward on l in front of r.

Beats: 1
& 2

Bar 4

4 Step back on r (short step) facing the line of dance and hop on r bending the l knee in front.

Beats: 1
& 2

Repeat these steps, working them up in speed and vigour.

The quaver leading into bar 17 may be counted as the last quaver of bar 16, and the bar between 16 and 17 omitted.

PENTOZALI

from CRETE

D.C.

KALAMATIANOS

Region	All regions of Greece; danced by men and by women. Plates 3 and 4 and others.	
Character	Slow and smooth, although the men, especially the leader, may vary the basic steps with springs and turns.	
Formation	A chain. The line progresses to the R, counter-clockwise.	

Dance	MUSIC *Bars and Rhythm*
Feet together, toes to centre.	1
1 Step to side on r, turning to L.	slow
Step back on l, backing the line of dance.	quick
Turning to face centre, step to side on r and hop on r turning to R to face the line of dance.	quick
	2
2 Step on l in front of r foot to face the line of dance.	slow
Step to side on r, turning to L.	quick
Step back on l, turning to back the line of dance.	quick
	3
3 Step to side on r, turning to R to face centre.	slow
Step on l in front of r foot to face the line of dance.	quick
Transfer weight back on r foot.	quick
	4
4 Step to side on l, turning to L.	slow
Step on r in front of l foot to back the line of dance.	quick
Transfer weight back on l foot.	quick

Repeat as often as desired. On step 1, beat 1, no turn to left is needed when dance is repeated.

Music Notes

The value of the slow and quick beats is as follows:

Slow = 3 beats
Quick = 2 beats.

If Parts 1 and 2 are used consecutively the quaver leading into Part 2 must be counted as the last beat of bar 16, and the bar of piano accompaniment between bars 16 and 17 must be omitted.

KALAMATIANOS

PART 1 Slow and smooth ♪=108

PART 2

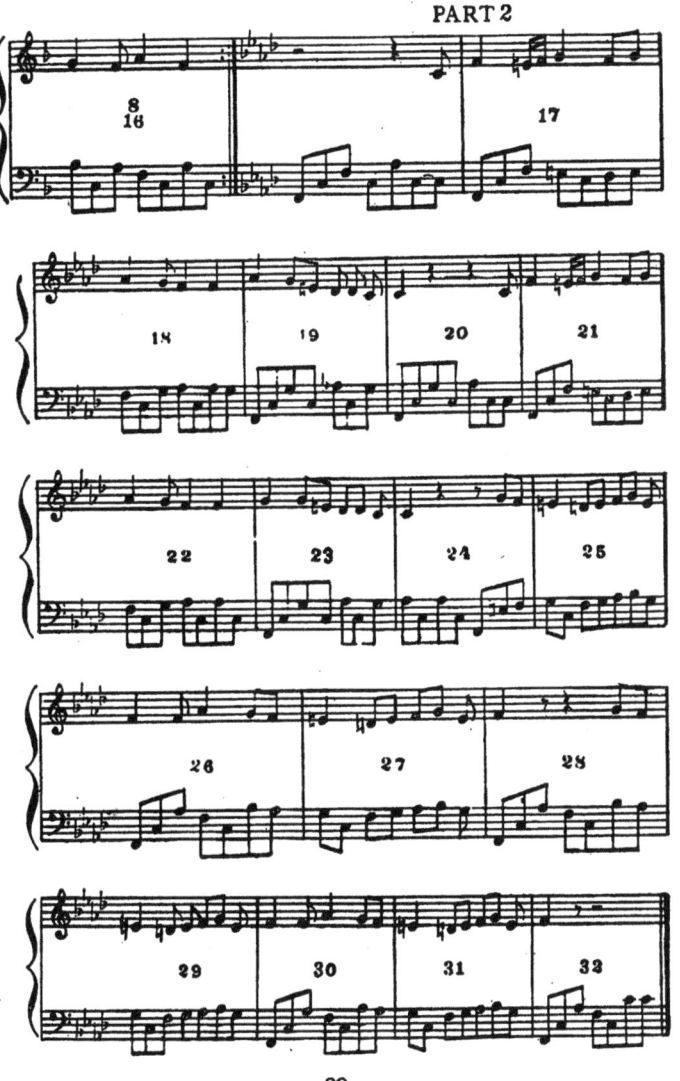

Plate 3
Amalia costume

Evzone costume

TSAMIKOS

Region All parts of Greece. Plate 1 and others.

Character When danced by women the steps are smooth. The men embroider the basic steps with turns, hops, heel points, and springs to full knee-bend position and up again. The Klephts or guerrillas give the steps a more stealthy quality.

Formation Chain. The leader often breaks away from the chain and performs skilled leaps and gymnastic feats. The dance moves first to R then to L but the progression is to the R, counter-clockwise.

Dance. Stand with r foot crossed in front of l foot.

Movement to R

1 Step to side on r.
  Step on l in front of r foot to face line of dance.

2 Point r foot forward on toe twice.
  Close r to l foot, taking weight on r foot.

3 Point l foot forward on toe and hold it for 2 beats.
  Step on l in front of r foot.

4 Step to side on r.
  Hop on r foot, bending l leg backward from the knee and turning head to look at foot.

MUSIC

Bar 1
Beats:
1–2
3

Bar 2
Beats:
1–2
3

Bar 3
Beats:
1–2

3

Bar 4
Beats:
1–2
3

TSAMIKOS

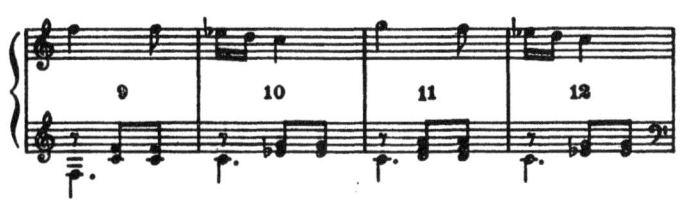

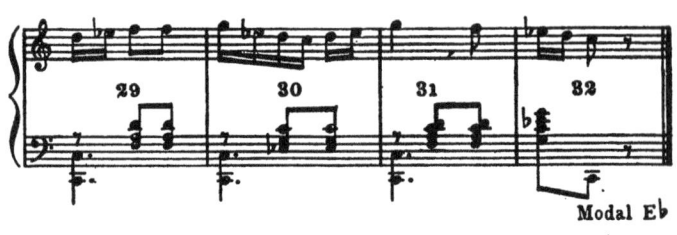

Modal E♭

Movement to L	*Bar 5* Beats:
1 Step to side on l.	
Step on r in front of l foot, turning to face L.	1–2 3
	Bar 6 Beats:
2 Step to side on l.	1–2
Hop on l foot, bending r knee up in front.	3
	Bar 7 Beats:
3 Step to side on r.	1–2
Step on l in front of r foot to face R.	3
	Bar 8 Beats:
4 Point r foot to side on toe.	1–2
Beat r foot in front of l and hold it for 2 beats.	3

Repeat these steps as often as desired working up the dance with hops, turns and beats.

N.B.—The head follows the body except when specially mentioned.

HASSAPIKOS (*Butchers' Dance*)

Region Originally from Constantinople. Was danced by Greek butchers on their feast-day. Plates 1, 3 and 4.

Character The rhythm is marked by clearly defined foot-beats and by a continuous bending and stretching of the knees which gives an undulating movement. The steps are very short and little ground is covered.

Formation Chain dance. May be danced by men only or by men and women alternately in one line. Dancers face the centre of the circle throughout with hands on shoulders of the next dancer. The general movement of the chain is to the R, counter-clockwise direction.

Dance. Start with feet together, toes to centre.

	MUSIC Bars and Rhythm
1 *Travel to R*	1–2
Pivot on both heels turning toes to R and bending both knees.	slow
Pivot on toes turning heels to R and bending both knees.	slow
Repeat the pivot on heels and on toes.	slow } slow
2 *Travel to R*	3–4
Step sideways on r foot.	quick
Short step forward on l foot.	quick
Close r foot behind l foot with a sharp beat.	slow
Short step forward on l foot.	quick

HASSAPIKOS

Slowly

Brush r heel on ground beside l foot.	quick
Raise r leg forward with a straight knee rising up and down on l foot.	slow

3 *Travel backward from centre* 5–6
Place r foot behind l foot with a slight inward and outward pivot on l foot. — quick / quick
Place l foot behind r foot with a slight inward and outward pivot on r foot. — quick / quick
Repeat with r and l feet. — 4 quicks

(The action is similar to that of a very smooth and unexaggerated Charleston.)

4 *Travel to R* 7–8
As step 2.
quick
quick
slow
quick
quick
slow

5 *Travel backward from centre after first 2 slow beats.* 9–12
Raise r leg and circle it forward. — slow
Place r foot in front of l foot, bending both knees to deep squatting position. — slow
Raise r leg and circle it backward. — slow
Place r foot behind l foot, bending both knees as before. — slow
Raise l leg and circle it backward. — slow
Place l foot behind r foot, bending both knees. — slow
Raise r leg and circle it backward. — slow
Place r foot beside l foot. — slow

6 *Travel to R* 6 pivots on heels and toes travelling to R as in step 1. 3 stamps—r, l, r, on the spot.	13–16 6 slow quick quick slow
7 *Travel to R* As step 2.	17–18 quick quick slow quick quick slow
8 *Travel backward from centre* As step 5, taking only 1 quick beat for each movement and with only slight knee-bending. Finish with feet together on last step.	19–20 8 quicks
9 *Travel to R* As step 2.	21–22 quick quick slow quick quick slow
10 *Travel backward from centre* 2 steps backward with slight knee-bending. Step sideways to R and close l foot slowly to r foot.	23–24 slow slow slow slow

BIBLIOGRAPHY

ALFORD, VIOLET, and GALLOP, RODNEY.—*The Traditional Dance*. London, 1935.

DAWKINS, PROFESSOR R. M.—*Journal of Hellenic Studies*, No. XXVI, p. 191.

HAGIMIHALI, ANGÉLIQUE.—*Skyros*. Art Populaire de l'Epire. Art Populaire Grec.

HAJI-COSTA, ISMENE.—"Some Traditional Customs of the People of Cyprus." *Folklore*, vol. LV, September 1944.

HUGHES, HILDA.—*The Glory that is Greece* (containing article on Greek Folk Songs and Dances by Lady Crosfield). London.

LAWSON, G. C.—*Annual of the British School at Athens*, No. VI.

PETRIDES, P. J.—*Greek Folklore and Greek Music*.

SAKELLARIOU, G.—*Fifty Greek Dances* (translated by Th. Stefanidi). Athens.

TARSOULI, ATHENA.—*Costumes Grecs*. Athens.

www.ingramcontent.com/pod-product-compliance
Lightning Source LLC
Chambersburg PA
CBHW061743290426
43661CB00127B/968